BRITAIN IN OLD P

# GRAVESEND & NORTHFLEET REVISITED

## ROBERT H. HISCOCK

The History Press

Digging slit trenches on the bank of Watling Street above the Tollgate, *c.* 1940. Back row, left to right: Phipps, Emmet and J. Beslee (with the spade). Front: J. Drysdale with the pick and R.H. Hiscock with pliers for revetment work. The trenches were dug too near the cutting face and would not have been protection against bullets, so they had to be filled in and dug again in solid chalk!

First published in 1998
This edition first published in 2009
Reprinted 2012

The History Press
The Mill, Brimscombe Port
Stroud, Gloucestershire, GL5 2QG
www.thehistorypress.co.uk

ISBN 978 0 7524 5043 8

Typesetting and origination by
The History Press
Printed in Great Britain

# CONTENTS

# ACKNOWLEDGEMENTS

First I must again express my thanks to those who, over many years, have given me illustrations and material relating to Gravesend and district. I hope they will think that I have made good use of it so that others may enjoy it or be induced to carry out research into local history. My apologies to anyone whose consent to use material ought to have been but was not obtained. It is difficult to trace the origins of some of the pictures.

Once more, I am indebted to the Gravesend Library for their help and assistance and their pictures are acknowledged. Also to some individual owners of material who have let me use items belonging to them and, again, I hope all these are acknowledged correctly.

In addition to the standard histories, i.e. Pocock, Cruden, Arnold, Mansfield and Philip, I have used E.R. Green's *Old Pubs and Breweries of the Gravesham Area* (1989) for information on public houses, as well as the numerous local guidebooks and directories.

I must also thank Sutton Publishing and, in particular, Simon Fletcher and Annabel Fearnley for all their help, and I must thank my daughter-in-law Mrs Denise Hiscock for typing this manuscript. I would also like to thank Philip Rothwell, one of the partners in my old firm, for lending me a collection of local directories going back to 1880, which are useful to refer to without having to go to the library collection whenever I needed to check something.

# INTRODUCTION

In 1988 I compiled a *Gravesend in Old Photographs* collection for Sutton Publishing, which is now out of print, and this was followed in 1990 by *Around Gravesham in Old Photographs*, which I produced jointly with Douglas W. Grierson and in which I compiled a section on Northfleet. Both these books proved popular and Sutton Publishing asked me to compile another volume on Gravesend and Northfleet. The chalk cliffs along the waterside from Botany Marsh and the Creek at Northfleet to the marshes at Denton really form a continuous whole and I have therefore included Northfleet in this collection.

I have followed the pattern of the first volume, namely to follow (1) the river, (2) the main road viz. Rochester Road, East Milton Road, Milton Road, King Street, New Road, Overcliffe, London Road, The Hill, Northfleet High Street and Stonebridge Hill, and (3) Old Road Gravesend from the Lion Garage, which continues as Dover Road to Northfleet to where it joins the main road at the Leather Bottle. In each case I have included some of the north–south roads to the south of my main lines but I have not included separate sections for the churches or local transport as I did in the first volume.

I must apologize for the quality of some of the illustrations. Whereas many areas have a large collection of views to choose from, some are just the opposite and there is only one view which will illustrate the point or contrast which I wish to make. I hope readers will overlook the poor quality of some views as they are unique and no other similar view is available as far as I am aware. I hope the captions will be of interest in recording aspects of the past which would otherwise be lost. In this way we can 'save and recover somewhat from the deluge of time', to use part of the quotation from the Advancement of Learning which appears opposite the title page in every volume of the Kent Archaeological Society's volumes of *Archaeologia Cantiana*.

There is I think no doubt that the origin of Gravesend and Northfleet derives from their position on the River Thames. Before the sea walls were built below the town this was the first place up river where there was firm ground beside the tideway for boats to land and embark and disembark passengers and cargo.

With the coming of the Romans and later the Normans, communication between London and the Continent became important. Travel by road was difficult and the long ferry between Billingsgate, London and Gravesend provided both an easier route for travellers and employment for the men of the town. Their rights to carry passengers from Gravesend to London were conferred on 'the men of the town' by Royal Charters, the earliest of which dates from 1401 and which referred to the rights as 'having subsisted from time where of the memory of man is not to the contrary!' The long ferry was at first a 'tide barge' depending on the tide and there were strict regulations as to times of departure, namely within twenty minutes of low tide to catch the flood from Gravesend and within twenty minutes of high tide to catch the ebb from Billingsgate. Otherwise the boat would not reach its destination before the tide turned and the passengers had to land and walk the rest of the way.

Sailing boats with a 'tilt' or awning were introduced in the sixteenth century and in due course replaced the barge. Early in the seventeenth century public coaches referred to as 'Tide Coaches' were introduced to meet the boats and to convey passengers to Dover and other towns in Kent – in 1647 the Corporation made regulations to deal with these. They were among the first stagecoaches in the country. In 1815 the first steam boat, the *Margery*, appeared on the long ferry and in due course they replaced the tilt boats, although small hatch boats for fish, market garden produce and general cargo continued, carrying a few passengers.

The coming of the steam boat resulted in a short 'Golden Age' for Gravesend as a summer holiday resort with the era of the Clifton Baths and Rosherville Gardens. However, the advent of the railway from London in 1849 gradually brought this to a close as people went farther afield for their holidays. The visitors' place was taken by commuters who travelled first by the steam boats for summer visitors and from 1849 all the year round by train.

The chalk cliffs near the river gave rise to the lime and cement trade. As early as 1168–9 lime was carried from Gravesend to Dover for work on the Castle by Henry II. Papermaking started with the building of the Imperial Paper Mills in 1911, followed by Bowaters in 1923, both now closed. Henley's Telegraph Works moved to Rosherville from Woolwich in 1906. Throughout the eighteenth and most of the nineteenth centuries ship-building was carried on – at Cleverley's yard from 1780 and at Pitchers at Northfleet from 1789 – and barges were built at Northfleet.

The river was important for transporting coal in from the Tyne and wood pulp for paper, and for exporting cement bricks and manufactured goods. Tilbury Docks opened in 1886 and this brought more work to the town. The river has ceased to be of such prime importance and the railways and now motor transport have enabled the town to become home to many commuters and a shopping and leisure centre, but the new container port at Tilbury and the import of coal and oil continue to be important.

It is hoped that the following series of views, showing the development of the town during the last 200 years or so, will be of interest to both old Gravesenders who will remember some of the scenes and also to newcomers who may wish to see something of the changes which have taken place here.

Readers will no doubt realize that the two east–west roads dealt with here are all different versions of the route from London to Dover or the Kent Coast, serving trade and communication with the Continent. The older and more numerous north–south roads, which can be traced sometimes as roads but sometimes now only footpaths, are evidence of an earlier way of life when flocks were grazed on the downs and then driven down to the lush waterside and marsh grazings for fattening and pigs were driven to Denns in the wealden woods to feed on the acorns and beechmast available in the autumn. This seems to have been an area where a fair amount of to-ing and froing has always taken place.

# CHAPTER ONE

# THE WATERSIDE

*Denton Mill, Denton Halt, Canal Basin, Sailing Club, Promenade, Gordon Gardens, Swimming Bath, Wates Hotel, Terrace Pier, Clarendon, Sailors' Mission, Crooked Lane, Amsterdam, Falcon, Town Pier, High Street, Market, Chapel Lane, St George's Church, Bath Street, Hospital, West Street Pier, Clifton Marine Parade, Yacht Club, Rosherville, Henleys, Cable Works, Power Station, Granby Road, Northfleet Cement Works, Hive House, The Creek.*

Denton Mill and the old Ship and Lobster from a drawing by Lott, 1812. The mill was built by Nicholas Gilbee in 1796. It had been pulled down by 1877. Nicholas Gilbee rebuilt Denton Court in 1791 and was an entrepreneur who built coal wharves at Denton, to avoid the coal tax, and also lime works. He married a Miss Cruden, sister of the historian, and went bankrupt in 1816.

Denton Halt. When the North Kent line was opened in 1849 there were no stations between Gravesend and Higham, but in 1906 a number of halts were built to cater for local traffic, including Denton. Only trains to Port Victoria and later Allhallows stopped at these and although the original wooden platforms were replaced by concrete in the 1930s they were closed in 1953 when the Allhallows service ceased. Denton Halt was peculiar – although it was on an electrified line only steam trains stopped there.

Albion Shades, *c.* 1900. E.W. Chapman was licensee.

Gravesend Model Yacht Club Regatta, 1909. Woodville Cottages in the background, built by Alfred Tolhurst, were said to be the first working-class cottages to have baths. They could be filled from the copper after the clothes had been washed first! For a number of years the Model Yacht Club was very popular and held annual regattas.

The old boathouse, *c.* 1890 (Gravesend Library). Built in about 1815 and demolished in 1942, it may have been the original of Charles Dickens' Peggotty's house at Yarmouth in *David Copperfield*. It had an upturned boat for a roof and upper storey.

The Gravesend and Rochester Railway. In 1845 a single line of railway was opened from the Canal Basin to Strood, running along the south side of the canal. Gravesend station was on the south side of the basin next to the gas works. Passengers left London by the London and Blackwall Railway, which was cable operated, and thence to Gravesend (Town Pier or Terrace Pier) by paddle boat. After travelling by train to Rochester (Strood), passengers for Chatham then proceeded again by boat or by horse vehicles to various parts of Kent. There are some timetables showing the connections in the Rochester Museum. The line was absorbed by the North Kent line in 1849. They filled in Strood tunnel and doubled the track and diverted it at Denton to the present Gravesend station.

Canal Basin, *c.* 1910 (J.A. Skellorn). The Canal Tavern electricity and gas works are in the background, with yachts and dinghies of Gravesend Sailing Club in the foreground.

Gravesend Sailing Clubhouse, 1905 (J.A. Skellorn). The Gravesend Sailing Club was formed in 1894, with headquarters at the Rosherville Hotel, for the local townsmen and youths who wanted to sail and for whom a club like the New Thames Yacht Club (see p. 59) did not cater. They moved to this site in 1905 when the clubhouse was built at the eastern end of the Promenade by subscription.

The interior of the Sailing Club, 1905 (J.A. Skellorn).

The entrance to the Gordon Gardens from Ordnance Road, *c.* 1905. The obelisk originally stood near the present eastern end of the Promenade and marked the limit of the Port of London, in which the coal tax was paid (see St George's Church, p. 37). It had replaced the old Round Tree which was formerly the marker. Wharfs at Denton did not pay this tax, and Ordnance Road which led to them was at one time known as the 'Free Coal Road'.

The Mayor, George Matthews Arnold, about to unveil the statue of General Gordon, 4 October 1893. He had given the gardens and extension of the Promenade as a memorial to General Gordon.

Gordon Gardens, *c.* 1914.

The Chantry and adjoining cottages, c. 1965. When Milton Chantry was taken over by the War Department as part of New Tavern Fort in 1779, the building was enclosed in a brick skin. This, along with the adjoining building, was removed from the east end in 1946 and a new window put in the original flint and rubble east wall, as seen here. The adjoining brick cottages were demolished in 1969 when it became apparent that the Chantry Chapel was a masonry crosswing of a large timber frame hall. In the background is the Customs House of 1816 and the Chantry Court to the left was built on the site of the Milton Tithe Barn, which was latterly used by the Corporation before being demolished by a V2 in 1944. The Chantry was equipped as a gas decontamination centre in 1938 and remained as such during the Second World War.

Fort House, c. 1890. At one time used by the Governor of the Fort, including General Gordon, and also one-time residence of the Town Clerk (Coombes), it was used as a school and later as a wartime food office. This building was also demolished by the V2 in 1944.

Promenade from Fort Gardens with shipping in the river, *c.* 1935.

Bandstand, Promenade, with Terrace Pier in the background, *c.* 1935. Concerts were held here before the opening of the Fort Gardens in 1932.

*Above:* The Gravesend Swimming Club, *c.* 1908. This was before the swimming bath was opened, when they swam in the river. Standing second from the left is Bertram Lovell, a local solicitor, and fourth from the left is James Benson, a one-time grocer, later a journalist with Odhams Press and a local historian.

*Left:* The 8th Earl of Darnley (top hat) with Princess Mary (?) and Chief Customs Officer (?) at the opening of the first public swimming pool, 31 August 1911. This occupied a site near the present Promenade Café. It was this Earl who, as the Hon. Ivo Bligh, brought back the 'Ashes' from Australia after the 1882–3 winter tour. The 'Ashes', some burnt bails in a small urn, were presented to him at the end of the tour by some Australian ladies, including his future wife, Florence Murphy. They were for many years exhibited at Cobham Hall. The Earl of Darnley was Lord High Steward of the Borough of Gravesend under the 1632 Charter.

The new open-air swimming pool was opened in 1938 in Ordnance Road and replaced the old swimming bath. It has in turn been replaced by the new baths in Thong Lane known as Cascades.

Wates Hotel, c. 1880 (Gravesend Library). This large weather-boarded structure was at the western end of the Promenade next to the Customs House, whose white lookout tower can be seen in the foreground. It was named after James Wate, its first proprietor in 1819. Charles Dickens stayed here when he was waiting to move into Gad's Hill Place. The eastern part (closed in 1925) was known as the Commercial Hotel. In 1886 the main building became the sailors' home and in 1918 the Sea School built new premises on the site. It was demolished in 1975 after the Sea School had moved to new premises on the marshes in 1967.

*Left:* The Customs House, built 1816, from the river with lookout on top: a fine stock brick building with Portland stone quoins and an interesting interior.

*Below:* The Terrace Pier and Gardens, 1845. The land, formerly belonging to the War Department, was sold to a company in 1835 who built a temporary pier and had pleasure gardens adjoining laid out by J.C. Loudon. The permanent pier illustrated here was opened in 1845. There was great rivalry between the Town and Terrace Piers, both of which went bankrupt. In 1852 a Receiver was appointed for the Corporation bondholders who ran the Town Pier (see pp. 28–9), the Town Hall and other Corporation property. The debts were not repaid until 1881, when the Town Hall was redeemed. The Terrace Pier appointed a Receiver soon after the Town Pier did.

The entrance to the Pier, *c.* 1900. The Terrace Pier was eventually acquired from the Receiver by a new company formed by the Pilots (who used the Pier as their headquarters) in 1893. They refurbished it (the work being done by E.A. & H. Sandfords) and sold the site of the gardens for housing. J.J. Robson, who was engineer of the 1914 Rochester Bridge, was the engineer in charge. Note the water tank over the left pavilion, a reminder of the fact that in its early days the Water Company only supplied water for certain hours of the day and storage tanks were necessary for a continuous supply.

The Terrace Pier from the riverside, 1925.

Amon Henry Wilds' proposals for the development of the area in 1830 included a pier with classical pavilions at its head, a bathing station with bathing machines and gardens, Harmer Street as built in 1834 but with a crescent on the south side of Milton Road as well as on the north, and the Grove continuing to the top of Windmill Hill. This drawing was exhibited at the RA in 1830 (No. 1038) entitled 'Town of Milton-on-Thames near Gravesend'.

The Gravesend Blockhouse and Governor's residence from an early nineteenth-century watercolour (Gravesend Library). The Gravesend Blockhouse was built in 1539 after Henry VIII's breach with Rome when invasion was feared. The buildings adjoining, now the Clarendon Hotel, were erected in about 1665 as a residence for the governor when the Duke of York, later James II, was appointed to the post of Lord High Admiral. The War Department let it to William Eagle, a member of the Corporation, in 1830 and finally sold it to John Chaplin of Rochester, who in 1842 converted it to a hotel and pulled down the Blockhouse. The Prince of Wales, later Edward VII, stayed here when waiting for Princess Alexandra to arrive at the Terrace Pier in 1863.

The Clarendon as a hotel, *c.* 1905. The row of cottages to the right were at one time occupied by a Mr Combers (known as 'Captain Silver'), who had a large collection of ship figureheads now in the *Cutty Sark*.

The foundations of the Gravesend Blockhouse were excavated by the Thameside Archaeological Group in 1975. They were under the Clarendon Lawn. The east side of the Blockhouse is under the car park and has not been excavated.

The Old Amsterdam, one of the many waterside inns with its own 'bridge' or landing place, *c.* 1880. The other entrance was from East Street. It was at the Amsterdam that the Corporation used to have breakfast after the annual Mayor making. Entries in their accounts 'to Amsterdam' at one time puzzled me as I could not understand why they went to Holland!

'Waiting for the Ferry.' When many years ago I saw a photograph of this painting by Tissot in the *Telegraph* I could not understand the title, because so far as I knew the ferry never ran from the Old Falcon, but I have recently learnt that it was allegorical. It is of Kathleen Newton, Tissot's mistress, who was dying at the time and she was waiting for the ferryman Charon to take her across the Styx to the underworld, with Tissot and their child waiting for her death.

Warner's Boat Builders, c. 1950. Between the Amsterdam and the King of Prussia (post-1914 the King of the Belgians) was a boatbuilder's, William Warner. This is the East Street side and the premises backed on to the river. Mr Warner's father, who served his time with Corbett's boatbuilding yard at Greenwich, started the business in what had been a fish shop in 1864 and produced a distinctive boat much favoured by Gravesend watermen, having seven planks aside instead of the usual six. One of these boats was given each year as a prize for the Apprentices Race in Gravesend Regatta. These premises, along with all those between East Street and the river, except the Three Daws, were demolished in 1954.

Crooked Lane, c. 1910. The buildings were demolished in the 1920s slum clearances, but the roadway remained as a narrow twisting carriageway until the ring road was constructed in 1958.

*Left:* The Founders Arms and top of Crooked Lane adjoining Queen Street, *c.* 1900. First licensed in 1860, it closed in 1904.

*Below:* The ring road, *c.* 1978. The shop on the left (since demolished) was where Queen Street joined Crooked Lane. The Three Daws can be seen to the centre with the Town Pier and Tilbury Landing Stage beyond. St Andrews Gardens running down to the waterside cover the sites of the Old Falcon, King of the Belgians, Warner's Boatyard, Amsterdam and Woods house and brewery, which were in East Street.

*Right:* The entrance from Queen Street to The Terrace, 1954.

*Below:* The corner of The Terrace looking up Queen Street towards the George on the corner of Terrace Street, 1954.

South side of The Terrace, 1954. Built in 1791 by James Leigh Joynes, it was the first row of houses and new street in the town to be constructed as a speculation. It replaced a footpath which led to New Tavern. The Terrace became part of the ring road west–east in 1958 and the houses were demolished in about 1970 and the present flats built.

Clarendon Cottages, *c.* 1925. These cottages were in a yard to the north of The Terrace and were said to be about 400 years old. They were once known as Grape Vine cottages and in the eighteenth century were the Milton Parish Workhouse. The bill of fare and rules and regulations concerning the workhouse in 1783 were printed from the Milton Vestry Book in the *Gravesend Historical Society Transactions* for 1972 (No. 18, p. 9).

*Right:* The Waterside Mission, *c.* 1868. The Revd C.E.R. Robinson, appointed vicar of Holy Trinity in 1861, was very concerned about the seamen and also immigrants and their children in boats on the river. He raised funds and bought an old waterside public house, the Spread Eagle, and used this together with a small launch to run a mission to seamen, supplying comforts and Bibles and tracts and christening children. This was his headquarters. The moored boats are bawleys engaged in shrimping – hence the name Bawley Bay.

*Below:* The Waterside to the east of the Town Pier, *c.* 1900, showing (right to left) the river frontage of Woods, East Street Brewery and St Andrew's. Built as a memorial to Admiral Sir Francis Beaufort KCB by his daughter Miss Beaufort, St Andrew's opened in 1871 (architect G.E. Street, the architect of the Law Courts in the Strand) as a chapel for the mission and the Clarendon Hotel. The mission later moved to Tilbury Docks, but the chapel continued in use until 1970 when it was acquired by the Corporation as an arts centre.

The temporary Tower Pier, c. 1833. In 1831 the Council decided to apply to Parliament for an Act to build a Town Pier so that the steam boats being used on the Long Ferry could come alongside to disembark passengers instead of mooring in the river and landing them by watermen's boats. A temporary pier was built, as seen here. The watermen bitterly opposed the bill and, when it was passed by the House of Lords on 22 June 1833, burnt the pier down.

The Tollhouse and railings at the entrance to the Pier, c. 1840. The railings were later moved to North and South House, Windmill Street (see p. 90).

The engineer of the new Town Pier was W.T. Clark and it was built by William Wood at a cost of £8,700. It was opened on 29 July 1834. This view of about 1905 shows it after it had been covered in by the railway company.

Entrance to the Town Pier, c. 1905. The London Tilbury and Southend Railway opened their line from Fenchurch Street to Tilbury in 1854 but it did not reach Southend until 1856. The Company's Act gave them powers to operate a steam ferry for rail passengers only to Gravesend and at first they used the Town Pier, paying a toll for each passenger. Disputes with the Corporation resulted in the construction of West Street Pier and for a time all the railway ferries used this. The company bought the Town Pier in 1884, having previously acquired the ferry rights, and from this date it became their Gravesend station and appeared as such in train timetables. The company was acquired by the Midland Railway in 1912.

The entrance to the Pier, *c.* 1925, after it had become part of the London Midland and Scottish Railway in 1923. Note the urinal on the left with fancy cast-iron roof.

The second ferry named *Tilbury* (from a painting in Gravesend Library) was built in 1883 by J. & K. Smit (Rotterdam) and the sub-contractor John Perin & Co. of Greenwich. It took the official party to Tilbury Docks for the opening in 1886. The ferry fleet in 1855 consisted of three paddle boats, *Earl of Essex*, *Earl of Leicester* and the first *Tilbury*, renamed *Sir Walter Raleigh* in about 1880. The first screw boat was the *Carlotta* in 1893, followed by the *Rose* in 1901 and the *Catherine* in 1903. The TSF *Tilbury* was broken up in 1922.

*Above:* Troops on exercise, crossing the river by barges being warped over by cables attached to buoys, 1779 (Gravesend Library).

*Right:* High Street from Town Pier Square, *c.* 1905. The Pier Hotel is on the right with the narrow entrance to West Street just beyond.

The International Tea Co. Stores, 17 High Street, *c.* 1905. This was one of the first multiple stores to open in the town, having taken over an existing tea store in about 1891. At the time it was the Indian Empire Tea Co. and had formerly been Hind Bros Tea Dealers. I do not know the names of the figures but the manager in 1905 was P. Cripps. The manager in 1891 was W. J. Godden.

John Rose and Co. Tailors, *c.* 1890. The short figure on the left is John Rose. The business continued as a limited company until about 1960.

*Right:* The old Town Hall, later used as a magistrates court (now closed and the branch amalgamated with Dartford). More recently the local museum was in the process of further change. The hall was built in 1764 by the local architect Charles Sloane to replace one of 1573. The classical front was added in 1836, the architect being Amon Henry Wilds, and the builder William Woods. The figures on the pediment were Minerva in the centre, with Justice on the right and Truth on the left. They were removed in 1939 in case of air raids dislodging them, but I have never been able to find what happened to them in spite of enquiries of the then borough engineer.

*Below:* The Borough Police Force (Gravesend Library). The date of this early photograph is unknown but is probably of 1870–80. The borough force was formed in 1836, the first Chief Constable being Mr Will Norton. The force was taken over by the Kent CC in 1941 under the war time legislation. This view was taken when three brick arches still supported the rear of the Council Chamber. There is now a rolled steel joist. The shops on the west side of High Street and the back of one of the Doric columns of the façade can be seen in the background.

The Borough Fire Brigade (Gravesend Library) – again undated but probably from about 1870–80. Gravesend was noted for its fires. *Punch*, on one occasion in the nineteenth century, had a paragraph headed 'No fires in Gravesend this week'. A disastrous fire in 1846, which destroyed a considerable amount of property at the lower end of High Street and in Town Pier Square (west side) and West Street, resulted in a town meeting requesting the Commissioners of Pavements and the Town Council to support a permanent fire brigade.

Gravesend market, *c.* 1830. In 1818 the Corporation entered into an agreement with Mr Charles Fowler to lay out a new market and this was the result. When the present market was built, the columns on either side were presented to the then Mayor, G.M. Arnold, who erected them on his estate at Milton Hall. They are now in the back garden of 30 Pine Avenue. The Town Hall with the three arches can be seen in the background. At a later date a fish market was built at the Queen Street end. Fowler was also responsible for Covent Garden and Hungerford Markets.

The entrance to the present covered market, which was built in 1898 (Ted Pook). The architect was Edmund J. Bennett and the builders Messrs Multon & Wallis, both local firms. The inscription records that the original grant of market rights was to Robert de la Parrock in 1268. The site of the market was part of the manor of Parrock which the Corporation acquired in 1694.

Opening the new market hall, 18 December 1898 (Gravesend Historical Society, photo D.W. Grierson). After a civic procession down High Street, led by the Band of the 1st Kent Volunteer Artillery under J. Watson, the party, with great difficulty because of the crowds, ascended a platform at the east end of the hall. In the front row are, from left to right, Alderman Geo. Butchard (engineer and cement maker), Alderman J. Hanks Cooper (furnisher and undertaker), G.M. Arnold, in uniform, Deputy Lieutenant of Kent. A retired solicitor, Arnold had been mayor from 1896 to 1897 but was never a member of the Corporate Body. In wig and bands is Charles Hatton, Town Clerk, the tall bearded figure is probably the Revd J.H. Haslam, rector of Gravesend, the Mayor in his chain of office and with the Mayor's Wand is John Russell the brewer. Also in the row is W.J. King, borough treasurer. The tall figure in the centre is Lt-Col. J.H. Saukey, commandant 1st Kent Volunteer Artillery. Also present are mace bearer, J.P. Jayne, and Alderman Payne.

Stall in the covered market, said to be Everden's, *c.* 1910.

St George's Church, 1890. It was built in 1732, after its predecessor was burnt down in 1727, with a grant of £5,000 out of the Coal Dues under the 1714 Act of Queen Anne for building fifty new churches. Gravesend was just within the coal due area (see p. 12). The architect was a local man, Charles Sloane, and the building agreement has been published in Philip's *History* (p. 132). The cost, excluding pews and spire, was £3,824. This picture shows the original shallow apse for the communion table. The last building to the left is Church Street School, built in 1875 as the first local 'boardschool', which closed in about 1975 and, after being used temporarily as the Magistrates Court, was demolished in 1979.

This view of St George's from the south-east, *c.* 1900, was used on the cover of the early church magazines. It was taken from the back window of a house in Wakefield Street.

*Above:* St George's choir outside the old (north) main door, *c.* 1890. Geo. R. Ceiley, the then organist, is in the centre.

*Right:* The new chancel and vestry from the north when built in 1892, before the north aisle was built in 1897. Architects for this work, as well as the 1897 North Aisle, were W. & C.A. Bassett-Smith, incorrectly called 'Mr Barrell Smith' in the faculty for the chancel.

Interior of St George's, showing the new chancel, which incorporated the stained glass and panelling from the old apse, c. 1893. The reredos has not yet been installed. From 1892 a cross appeared on a rear table, or gradine, behind the altar.

With the building of the North Aisle in 1897 the north and south galleries were removed and the rector, the Revd J.H. Haslam, painted the Nativity on the east nave wall (north) and the Crucifixion (south). These paintings were replaced in 1914 by windows presented by the Colonial Dames in memory of Pocahontas. The reredos is now in place. The angels in the roof were painted from lantern slides and two angels painted by Mrs Fletcher, the wife of William Fletcher, churchwarden, were attached to the communion rail newels. These are still there.

A close-up of the east end just before the church was closed for regular worship in 1952. The very fine 1892 Clayton & Bell reredos (somewhat marred in this view by flowers!) was discarded in 1968 when the church once more became the parish church of Gravesend and the interior was re-ordered and the open sittings replaced by chairs. The reredos is said to be still in the church.

*Above:* The churchyard, 1957, just before the tombstones were cleared in that year. Westside Place (in the background) was demolished in 1964. Church Street School is the high building at the rear. The obelisk of the Arnold tomb (left) survives.

*Left:* In 1958 the Corporation renamed the churchyard 'Pocahontas Gardens': a bronze statue of the princess was presented by the people of Virginia and unveiled in a torrential downpour of rain by the Governor, Mr John S. Battle. Pocahontas was buried under the chancel of the previous church when she died on a visit to England in 1616.

The Cruden Tomb just before it was demolished, 1957. Robert Pierce Cruden, the historian, was buried on 6 November 1847 and his daughter Maria, who was also interred in this tomb, was the last person to be buried in the churchyard, in 1909.

The Salt Box, Bath Street, *c.* 1910. The last thatched building in the town, it was demolished in the 1920s slum clearances. In 1851 it was used as a Sunday School by the Gravesend Ragged School, which later occupied an adjoining building in Clifton Road.

*Left:* Princess Street Congregational Chapel shortly before it was demolished in 1961 to make way first for a car park and then Marks & Spencer. The congregation moved to Old Road East in 1953 and is now at St Paul's United Reform Church, Singlewell Road. It was the third chapel to occupy this site and was built by John Gould in 1838.

*Below:* During demolition of the chapel in 1961 a number of bodies of prominent members were found under the site of the pulpit, which was in the centre under the arch shown here.

Gravesend's first gas works, built in 1824 on the west side of Bath Street. The town was first supplied with gas on 9 December that year. There were problems with expanding on this site and the undertaking moved to the site near the Canal Basin in 1843.

Although the works were demolished, the podium and retaining wall on which it was built remained until the new ring road was built. Here it is seen shortly before removal for the new road in 1967. The site was occupied by Crescent Trading Co., builders' merchants.

*Left:* Chapel Lane, *c.* 1914. This short lane led from opposite the north door of St George's Church to West Street and is said to have derived its name from the Chapel of Ease built on the site of the present church in 1492. The weatherboard building on the left, which had a frontage to Church Street, was at one time the Gravesend post office.

*Below:* West Street from Church Street, 1978. Chapel Lane is the paved pathway on the right. To the left with the bow window is the Three Crowns, with the three crowns in brick above the window. This was the old Cross Ferry landing place. Next to it behind the trees was the car and goods ferry landing stage now used by the passenger ferry. Next to this is the New Falcon (previously the Rhum Butt, 1789–1811, the Rum Puncheon, 1811–44, and the Talbot, 1844–9).

*Right:* The original Gravesend Hospital in Bath Street. The site was given by the Earl of Darnley in 1853 and this building was erected by John Gould, a local architect and builder, in 1854. It was incorporated in the present building and its side wall can still be traced on the left-hand side of the approach to the old main entrance.

*Below:* The ladies' ward in the hospital, *c.* 1905.

Clifton Road, *c.* 1967. Truman's bottling plant and stores are on the right, with the high roof of the Terminus Hotel in the background. This was at one time the end of the turnpike road to Northfleet which became dangerous because of quarrying and, after use was made of Dover Road, Old Road West and Pelham Road, it was replaced by the New Road, Overcliffe and London Road in 1801.

Flint Cottages in Moscow Road just before demolition, 1972. A number of flint cottages and houses were built in the nineteenth century using Portland cement and brick facings. Flint is not a very satisfactory building material although it was cheap locally as a waste product of chalk quarrying for lime and cement.

The New Falcon Hotel (waterside), *c.* 1898. This was famous for its whitebait suppers in the long glazed restaurant overlooking the river and was at one time the venue for mayoral banquets. It became the New Falcon Laundry in about 1906. Its proprietor, Mr John Meggy, was a well-known local character, nicknamed 'Mr Pickwick'. The laundry closed here in 1960 and the premises were demolished in 1972. The goods and later car ferry landing place is the building to the right.

The Three Crowns bridge or causeway, 1922. This was the original landing place for the cross ferry to Tilbury. The shore to the right is one of the supports for the pontoon for the car ferry (now the landing place of the passenger ferry).

An aerial view of Gravesend and the Waterside, 1964 (*Kent Messenger*). In the background on the left are the Promenade and Canal Basin; on the right, Milton Road and Park Place. The Fort Gardens are below the trees with the then new blocks of Chantry Court. New Bridge can be seen, with moored boats, as well as the Terrace Pier, with pilot cutter. The Three Daws, St Andrew's and the Clarendon can be seen beside the river, with Crooked Lane rising up to The Terrace. One of the new diesel passenger ferries, introduced in 1961, can be seen at the Town Pier and either the *Mimie* or the *Tessa* at the West Street car ferry pier. They were withdrawn and scrapped after the car ferry service closed at the end of 1964. The passenger service was transferred to this pier and the Town Pier was sold. St George's Church stands in the centre with Church Street Schools and the houses still in Bath Street and Wakefield Street. Two water boats are moored at Crawley's Wharf, and the Railway Pier and the West (formerly 'Street') station and yard are in the foreground.

Orient Pacific RMS *Ormuz* at Tilbury Tidal Basin, with a paddle tug, 1889. Tilbury Docks opened in 1886 and the Orient Pacific moved their Australian mail service to Tilbury in 1889, this being their first mail boat to call there.

The P&O liner *Strathmore* at Tilbury landing stage, *c.* 1938. The landing stage and the new Tilbury Riverside station with direct access to the stage were opened in May 1930 by the then Prime Minister Ramsay Macdonald. The P&O SS *Magnolia* was the first vessel alongside. In the background can be seen the Tilbury Hotel, burnt down by a bomb in the Second World War, the Tidal Basin and old entrance to the docks with various ships loading and unloading in the docks.

The Tilbury ferry *Rose, c.* 1960. It was built in 1901 by A.W. Robertson & Co. *London* was only the second screw ferry, the first being the *Carlotta*, built in 1893. The *Rose* and her sister ship, the *Catherine* of 1903, survived until 1961 when they were replaced by diesel boats and scrapped. They were said to be the last passenger-carrying boats on the Board of Trade register to be lit by oil. The boat at the Tilbury landing stage would appear to be the last of the Orient line mail boats, *Himalaya*, before the line to Southampton was removed in 1969.

The *Crested Eagle, c.* 1930. Most of the Thames pleasure boats from London to Southend, Margate and Ramsgate, or Clacton called at Tilbury landing stage or the West Street Railway Pier and were popular with Gravesend day-trippers. The *Crested Eagle* was the first of the General Steam Navigation Company's boats to be oil fired and originally had a telescopic funnel and mast to enable her to pass under London Bridge when the service started from Old Swan Pier. Later Tower Pier was used and the telescopic funnel became redundant. She was built by J. Samuel White and Co., Cowes. She went to Dunkirk where she was bombed and caught fire and was totally destroyed. A motor vessel built after the war later bore her name.

The boat train at Gravesend West Street station, 1938 (by the late H.C. Casserley *per* Richard Casserley). Between the wars the Batavia line, which maintained a mail and goods service between London and Rotterdam, called at the Railway Pier to pick up passengers who had travelled by train from Victoria. The boat train usually consisted of four carriages with headboards pulled by an 0–4–4 tank or as here by an 0–6–0 goods engine. Sir Neville Henderson, the last ambassador to Nazi Germany, records, in his book *Failure of a Mission*, landing here on his return after the outbreak of war in September 1939. He and his staff had to carry their own baggage because of a complete absence of porters – a not unusual state of affairs at West Street Station.

The entrance to Gravesend West (the 'Street' was dropped by British Rail in 1950) when the line was finally closed to goods traffic, *c.* 1968. The passenger service, long since reduced to five trains a day except for the Saturday afternoon push-and-pull, had ceased in 1953. The line had been opened on 17 April 1886, the same day as Tilbury docks. After opening the line, the official party crossed in one of the ferries to inspect the docks.

The demolition of Gravesend West station, 1987 (Miss J. Barnes). The pier remains and was used by Clifton Slipways and others for mooring and repairing boats.

A Gravesend hatch boat double reefed, from a drawing by E.W. Cooke, 1828 (Dr P.H.G. Draper). The wharf to the right is probably the old Red Lion Wharf with Sheeps Hill behind and Rosher's lime works quarries. To the left is a paddle boat making for Gravesend and the spire of St George's Church can be picked out, as can the windmill on Windmill Hill. The hatch boats used for fishing had a central wet tank to take the fish up to Billingsgate and they were also used for general cargo.

Thames barges making up the river with Tilbury Fort in the background, c. 1905. The Thames barges could be handled by a man (the skipper) and a boy or young man (the mate) and were an economical means of transport for heavy cargoes such as lime, cement, bricks and coke as well as agricultural produce. Large fleets were owned by the cement and brick works, as well as by general carriers such as Everards of Greenhithe and London & Rochester Trading of Rochester. The last commercial barges were those used by ICI at their explosives wharf at Denton.

*Right:* A hay barge, *c.* 1900 (Gravesend Historical Society from a watercolour by the late A.T. Nash who designed the Gravesend Borough Oar). The sails were lifted up above the haystack, completely obstructing the view of the skipper at the tiller, who had to rely on the mate on top of the hay for steering instructions.

*Below:* The Clifton Baths, *c.* 1830. Bathing machines were introduced at Margate in 1753 by a Quaker, Benjamin Beale, and in May 1796 forty-nine local inhabitants joined in a subscription of five guineas each to found a Bathing Establishment at Gravesend. They purchased a machine at Margate which was used for the first time on 27 June 1796.

A view from the river of the first baths at Gravesend, with three bathing machines which were lowered and hauled up on brick runners by a winch; those in Thanet had a horse. When in the water the canopy was let down and one bathed discreetly under it. According to the guide from which the plate comes (1824), the charges were as follows: 'Warm Bath 3/- or 8 for £1.1.0, Cold ditto £0.1.0, Shower Bath £0.1.0, Machine £0.1.0'. In 1843 there were nine machines at Gravesend.

The new Clifton Baths (Gravesend Library). In 1834 a new oriental-style covered swimming bath was opened adjoining the original weatherboarded building, which can be seen to the left. This was followed by the Clifton Hotel, the building to the left, built by Mr Pallister who at one time owned the Old Falcon and built the riverside New Falcon.

*Right:* The interior of the Clifton Baths, *c.* 1860. According to the late Mr J. Benson it was always very cold as the sun did not get to it and in his time it was not heated. The last bath attendant was William Henry Jordan. They closed and became derelict in about 1900.

*Below:* Clifton Marine Parade at the time of the Great Frost, 1893 (Gravesend Library). The New Thames Yacht Club was founded as a breakaway from the Royal Thames Yacht Club in 1867 and in 1869 it absorbed the Union Yacht Club which had taken over Pallister's Clifton Hotel as its headquarters in about 1863. It continued here until about 1900. During the First World War the building was used as a VAD hospital and was afterwards acquired by the Imperial Paper Mills and demolished in 1938. To the left of the Yacht Club can be seen the Clifton Shades, a public bar known locally as the 'Wheelhouse', which continued until 1938, and to the right are the Baths and Clifton Terrace.

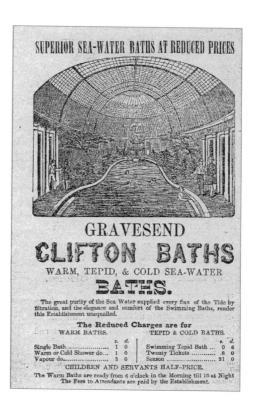

SUPERIOR SEA-WATER BATHS AT REDUCED PRICES

GRAVESEND

## CLIFTON BATHS

WARM, TEPID, & COLD SEA-WATER

### BATHS.

The great purity of the Sea Water supplied every flux of the Tide by filtration, and the elegance and comfort of the Swimming Baths, render this Establishment unequalled.

**The Reduced Charges are for**

| WARM BATHS. | | | TEPID & COLD BATHS. | | |
|---|---|---|---|---|---|
| | s. | d. | | s. | d. |
| Single Bath | 1 | 0 | Swimming Tepid Bath | 0 | 6 |
| Warm or Cold Shower do | 1 | 0 | Twenty Tickets | 8 | 0 |
| Vapour do | 3 | 0 | Season | 21 | 0 |

CHILDREN AND SERVANTS HALF-PRICE.
The Warm Baths are ready from 6 o'clock in the Morning till 10 at Night
The Fees to Attendants are paid by the Establishment.

*Above:* Schooners racing at Gravesend (Dr P.H.G. Draper), from the *Illustrated London News*, 1865. This shows the *Gloriana* (133 tons) winning the Thames Yacht Club Race in June 1865.

*Left: Britannia*, 1893 (J. Skellorn). The *Britannia* was built for HRH the Prince of Wales (later King Edward VII) in 1893 at the Clyde shipyard of D.W. Henderson. The designer was G.L. Watson. She was brought round to Gravesend in April and took part and won the first race of the season on 20 May. The Kaiser's yacht *Valkirie* was second (she broke her bowshirt in the Lower Hope).

Clifton Terrace and the Clifton Baths, c. 1890. Behind the trees at the top of the bank was Grove Cottage, at one time the residence of Alderman Ditchburn who had a ropery, and 'Rope Walk' was the name of a row of cottages at the back of the baths. William and Henry Ditchburn were mayors in 1837 and 1828 respectively.

The Hit or Miss public house and Fletcher's chalk and lime wharf, c. 1900. This was the area of the earliest chalk diggings and lime was supplied from Gravesend for Henry II's work on Dover Castle in 1168–9 (Pipe Rolls). William Cleverley started boat-building here in 1780 which was carried on by his son-in-law, Col. Gladdish. He was followed by William Fletcher who carried on the lime works and also imported coal and timber. All three lived at a house built by Cleverley and latterly called Bycliffes, behind trees just to the right of this picture.

Bycliffes Row or Slaves Alley (photograph by the late Dr R.A. Freeman) where the chalkies employed by William Fletcher lived, *c.* 1900. They had formerly lived in caves in the chalk cliffs. Above can be seen the backs of the houses in Pier Road, Northfleet, on top of the chalk cliffs.

*Right:* An aerial view of the waterside, *c.* 1925.
The Imperial Paper Mills purchased Bycliffes
and the adjoining quarries and lands in 1909
and built their mills in 1911. The works and
wharf can be seen in the centre of the picture,
with Clifton Marine Parade running through it.
At the bottom of the picture on the left can be
seen the old Yacht Club. This was later acquired
by the mills. Beyond, the trees cover the old
Rosherville Gardens with Henley's Cable Works
at the extreme top of the picture. The Imperial
Paper Mills closed in 1981 and the site is now
Imperial and Business Retail Park: Asda was the
first store to open on 7 November 1988.

*Below:* Landsdowne Square, Rosherville, *c.*
1925. It was laid out as part of H.E. Kendall's
Rosherville New Town in the 1830s and in the
centre was the entrance to the former pier to
which the trippers to Rosherville Gardens came.
At one time some of the ferries from Tilbury
came here to collect and return commuters
from Rosherville, who used the Fenchurch
Street–Tilbury line.

The west side of Landsdowne Square, showing the old Rosherville Hotel just before demolition, 1963. It had been used as a VAD hospital in the First World War and was then let out in flats and rooms. In its heyday visitors (including the future Edward VII) stayed here for the Gravesend Yacht week.

Crete Hall, *c.* 1820. This was a waterside house, built on land from which the chalk had been quarried by Benjamin Burch in about 1800. It was later occupied by his son-in-law, Jeremiah Rosher, a member of the family who ran the adjoining lime works and gave their name to Rosherville. This is a view of the front or south side with its miniature park. The masts and sails of ships on the river can be seen either side of the left-hand pavilion. The present Coach Road was the private drive leading from London Road, where there was a lodge, to the house.

The same area, 1925 (Gravesend Library). In the foreground are the trees of the derelict Rosherville Gardens and the Amalgamated Press, built in 1891 on the site of a house known as Old Crete Hall. Next are the original buildings of Henley's Cable Works built in 1906 on Crete Hall Park. The house and the right-hand pavilion can be seen in front, then used as his residence by the manager, Oliver Wright, and later as a canteen and offices before its demolition in 1938. Beyond the rest of Henley's are the derelict Red Lion cement works of 1896, the Deep Water Wharf and the eastern end of the 1924 Bowaters Paper Mills.

The Northfleet power station, c. 1955. The site of the Red Lion works was cleared during the Second World War and the Maunsell forts were built here. After the war in 1951 the Electricity Generating Board built this coal-fired generating plant on the site. This closed in 1991 and the chimneys were felled and the site cleared in 1994. It has not yet been redeveloped, although there are various plans for this site.

Granby Road, Northfleet, c. 1820. Howard House, on the left, was built in 1717. The houses near the river were for the shipwrights at Pitchers Dockyard, which was to the right. The tall building housed a stationary engine for pulling trucks between the brickfield to the right and the wharf. To the right is the corner of Caleybank, a huge unquarried chalk mass removed in 1955 when Bowaters was extended.

Looking across the site of the derelict London Portland cement works, *c.* 1923. This is now the site of New Northfleet works. The chimneys of Bevans works can be seen to the left.

Northfleet, *c.* 1830 (from Tumbleson's *Views of the Thames and Medway*). This view shows what is probably the rear of the Old India Arms public house.

Bevans Wharf, *c.* 1926. Bevans works were rebuilt in 1926, largely for the export trade, the deep-water channel of the river being near the south bank here. This view shows the deep-water wharf for unloading coal for the coal-fired kilns and exporting cement, which could be loaded direct into the ships' holds.

Shoeing horses which were used for hauling trucks at Bevans works, *c.* 1910.

An aerial view of Northfleet from the south, showing Tilbury town and Tilbury Docks in the background, with the two chimneys of the New Northfleet cement works on the side of the river and Bowaters Paper Mills to the right, *c*. 1978 (Blue Circle Industries). In the foreground is the Northfleet council estate of 1926 and at the bottom of the picture are the Springhead Road quarry and lake and the round settling tanks of the Northfleet sewage works.

Loading cement by night at the New Northfleet cement works, 1978 (Blue Circle Industries). This replaced Bevans works in 1970. Beyond can be seen the chimneys of the Northfleet power station (see p. 66).

Northfleet Creek, c. 1905. It was here that James Parker manufactured Roman cement under a patent of 1791. He had a 'Terrass' mill here. Roman cement was later made by White & Frost at Swanscombe and used for Brunel's Thames Tunnel, which was completed in 1843. Aspdin had a kiln near here (now preserved) where he produced Portland cement, but his business failed and was taken over by Robins who used the creek. Later Robins works were taken over by Knight Bevan & Sturge and became part of Bevans works.

# CHAPTER TWO

# THE MAIN ROAD

This chapter covers the main road (A226) and roads to the south, between it and Old Road (B261). Walker & Son's Maltings Chalk, Denton Church ruins, Milton Church, Park Place, Trinity Church, Milton Road, Clock Tower, The Grove, St John's Church, King Street, Windmill Street, Milton Congregational Church, Windmill Hill (for Old Prince of Orange, see Old Road), Stone Street, Wrotham Road, New Road, Garden Row, Rosherville, Leather Bottle, The Hill, Northfleet, St Botolph's Church, Northfleet High Street, Huggens College, New Northfleet Paper Mill, Tramway Company's buses.

The Malting's, Chalk, *c.* 1890. These belonged to Walker & Son's brewery (see p. 76), later Charringtons, and are now used as the Maltings Workshops. The maltings have now been demolished, and a technical college erected on the site.

The ivy-covered ruins of St Mary's, the original parish church of Denton in the grounds of Denton Court, *c.* 1900. The ruins were the inspiration for Canon Richard Barham's 'Ingoldsby Abbey' (see his note to 'The Ingoldsby Penance – A Legend of Palestine' in *The Ingoldsby Legends*) where 'a full choir of Monks and a full choir of Nuns shall live upon cabbage and hot cross buns'. He was a nephew by marriage of Col. Dalton (and one of his executors) who lived at Parrock House, now the flats in Joy Road, at which he stayed from time to time. G.M. Arnold of Milton Hall bought Denton Court and rebuilt the church, incorporating the ruins in 1901. It is now a Roman Catholic chapel. The architect for the restoration was J.A. Walters FSA. There never was an abbey here and 'Ingoldsby Abbey' was a fiction of Canon Barham.

*Right:* Milton parish church of St Peter and St Paul from the west, *c.* 1890. A fourteenth-century single cell building (the tower and south porch being slightly later), it had a drip eaves roof added in 1790 by Messrs Hall of Dartford, which Robert Pocock, Gravesend's first historian writing in 1797, said 'makes it appear more like a Chinese than an English Place of Worship!'

*Below:* The north side of Milton church, from a watercolour painting by G. Wheeler of 11 Garrick Street. It is undated but the fact that the Church Schools and Victorian rectory can be seen beyond the railway suggests that it is probably from about 1865. The figure in the foreground is on the footpath which led from Gravesend High Street along what is now Bank Street and East Terrace across the recreation ground (formerly the Captain's field) to Norfolk Road and Tunnel Arch under the railway to the church.

The eastern end of Park Place, 1954. It was built in about 1834 as part of the Milton Park Estate and it has been suggested that the name came from Mungo Park, the explorer, whose brother Dr Adam Park was associated with the development company. It seems more likely to have taken its name from the Milton Park Estate Company. The estate was laid out by A.H. Wilds. The houses, which had their own private drive, were demolished in 1957 when the council erected the present flats.

Holy Trinity Church at the junction of Milton Place and Ordnance Road, c. 1890. Built in 1844 with the help of a small grant (£600) under the Second Parliamentary Grant from Church Buildings Acts of 1818 and 1824, the church occupied a site given by the War Department. The total cost was £4,200 and the architect was J. Wilson. It was intended to have a spire but started with four pinnacles which appear in two early prints. These seem to have been removed, as shown here, but were restored by the early years of the twentieth century. It was demolished in 1963 after problems with the inferior ragstone and the congregation moved to St George's. It was at one time the fashionable church in the town, being supported by the pilots and waterside community.

Holy Trinity School dressed to represent 'India' for the Coronation celebrations of George V in 1911. It was treated as a 'Festival of Empire' and all the local Elementary and Church Schools took part, each representing a different part of the Empire. Holy Trinity Schools were built next to the church in 1865 at the expense of the vicar, the Revd C.E.R., and Mrs Robinson. The architect was G.E. Street and the schools were described as 'well built and ventilated, lighted with gas and thoroughly warmed by two open fires'. In 1962 they were burnt down but temporary accommodation was immediately provided at the barracks and when the barracks were closed a new school was built there. It is now the only Church primary school in the town.

The Globe, *c.* 1890. On the corner of Milton Road and Milton Place, it opened in 1824. It was opposite Holy Trinity Church and at least two of the church's organists always had a pint ready on the bar to consume during the sermon. The hanging lamp can also be seen in the picture of the church (p. 74).

*Left:* Walker & Sons brewery, Wellington Street, *c.* 1893. Alexander Walker appears as 'Brewer' at 10 Wellington Street in 1854 but by 1893 the business was run by 'the Trustees of Alexander Walker'. Charrington & Co. took over the business in 1905. In 1928 an extensive fire at Barton's timber yard caused the brewery to close and the premises were demolished in 1936. The site is now part of the Jolly Drayman, previously the Brewery Tap and locally known as the Coke Oven, in Love Lane.

*Below:* The south side of Milton Road junction with Wellington Street, *c.* 1890. The house on the corner, No. 133, was used as the first hospital or dispensary from 1850 until the erection of the premises in Bath Street in 1854, its object being 'to assist the really destitute poor of Gravesend and Milton and vicinities: unable to pay for medical aid'. At No. 137 lived George Newman, a local poet who was awarded the Bardic Title of 'Lloegryn' and who had a shop opposite. Herbert Austin, a well-known butcher, lived at No. 136 and at No. 139 lived Thomas Terry Chapman, Conservative agent and solicitor. In the 1860s Charles Crafter, son of William Crafter the local historian and 1st Ruler of Pilots, lived in this row. The row was demolished in 1961 and a garage now occupies the site.

*Above:* Milton Road looking west, *c.* 1925. The building on the right is the British Tar of 1808. The front of the upper storey is covered with mathematical tiles, i.e. imitation bricks to avoid the brick tax, and is the only example I know of these in Gravesend, although there are many elsewhere in Kent, e.g. Tenterden, Cranbrook and Canterbury. The lower storey is brick and the rear weatherboard, a curious example of use of different materials – perhaps it was built of 'job lots'! The large building on the left at the corner of The Grove is the post office, which moved here in 1842. The tower of St John's Roman Catholic Church, constructed in 1873 by Goldie & Child, and the spire of the Methodist Church, built in 1906 by Messrs Morley & Sons of Bradford are opposite each other.

*Right:* The Clock Tower, *c.* 1930 (D. W. Grierson). This tower was built in 1887 as a memorial to Queen Victoria's Golden Jubilee at a total cost of £1,097. The architect was John Johnson, who with Alfred Meeson was architect of the Alexandra Palace. To the left can be seen one of the twenty-seater Dennis buses of the Gravesend & District Bus Company, which operated a service from here to Perry Street from 1925, and later to Waterdales via Darnley Road.

The northwest corner of The Grove, *c.* 1890. This was occupied by H.G. Woodford Wine & Spirit Merchant, which later moved to Parrock Street and was taken over by Russells, later Trumans. There were extensive cellars beneath street level. Note the horse with a loaded barrel dray. The building later became the National Provincial Bank, with the North Kent Club above.

A view of The Grove, looking north with trees and homes on both sides, *c.* 1890. At one time called Upper Harmer Street, it originally had gates at both ends and was a private road.

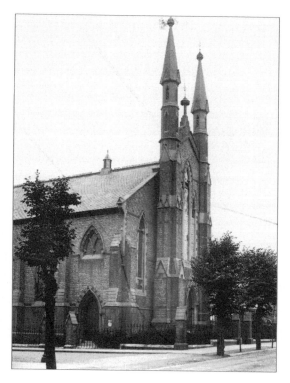

St Andrew's Presbyterian Church, *c.* 1890.
Before it was built in 1870, the congregation had
worshipped in the Town Hall. It cost £5,000. The
architect was Alfred Bedborough of Southampton.
It was demolished in 1965, having previously lost
one spire said to be unsafe, and the congregation
then joined the Congregational Church and
built the United Reform Church of St Paul in
Singlewell Road, to which some of the stained
glass was removed.

The butcher's shop and residence of R.J. Beamish
at the junction of The Grove with Parrock Street,
*c.* 1890. The architect was again John Johnson.
R.J. Beamish came from Wallington in Surrey and
after learning his trade settled in Gravesend and
purchased an old-established business from a Mr
Hicks, becoming the leading butcher in the town.
He was a churchwarden at Christ Church and a
leading freemason and founder of the Beamish
Lodge. The business was later carried on by J.
Robson.

The children of Christ Church School outside their school in Russell Street, representing British South Africa in the School's parade for the Coronation of George V, 1911.

Colonial troops, in London for the Coronation of 1911, on a visit to Gravesend, obstructing the passage of a tram in Milton Road en route for Swanscombe. The lower shops on the left with dormer windows were originally all part of the New Inn, which had a bowling green and 'fields', known as the 'New Inn Fields', in the space between the inn and the Methodist Church, by this time occupied by the taller shops and Berkley, Bernard and Wilfred Streets.

A four-horse cart of A. & H. Hardy, the Northfleet carriers, ready for an outing from the New Inn, Milton Road, *c.* 1900 (Gravesend Library). Rigdens were the Faversham brewers. The New Inn with the shops adjoining was originally the home of the Holker family where in April 1734 Dr Holker entertained the Prince and Princess of Orange (daughter of George II) after their marriage, when they were weatherbound on their return to Holland.

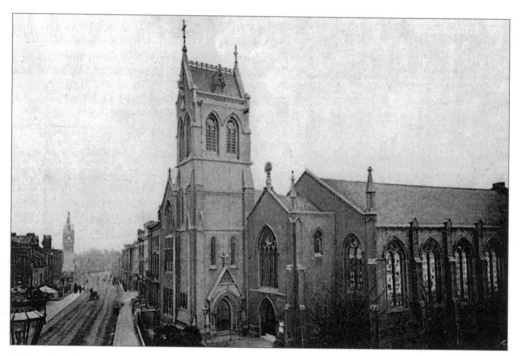

St John's Church, *c.* 1890. Built in 1834 (architect William Jenkins junior) as an Anglican Proprietary Chapel, it was sold in 1842 to the Revd W. J. Blew, curate of St Anne's, Westminster, who ministered here until 1851. After trouble with the Bishop of Rochester he sold the church to the Roman Catholics, although he himself remained an Anglican. Its Anglican patron saint was St John the Baptist, but the Roman Catholics changed this to St John the Divine.

The interior of St John's, *c.* 1868. The church was built with galleries which were removed at some date after 1860, but the shallow pilaster buttresses were not sufficient to support the roof and in 1912 six pairs of columns and wooden beams were inserted.

The Mitre Tavern, King Street, just before demolition in 1971. It had previously been the Pelican, 1794–1804, and then the Duke of York, 1804–35. The corner of the New Inn can also be seen on the other side of Queen Street.

King Street looking east, *c.* 1830. The timber-jettied building on the left is the Free School founded by the Corporation in about 1580 and further along on the same side can be seen the Mitre. On the right are the weatherboarded St Thomas' Almshouses, given to the town under the will of Henry Pinnock in 1624 and added to by James Fry in 1710. Their name derives from the fact that a pond known as St Thomas' waterings occupied the site at the junction of what are now King Street and Windmill Street. King Street was at one time known as Holy Water Street and later as St Thomas' Street.

King Street School, *c.* 1880. In 1835 the Free School was amalgamated with the National School associated with St George's Church (founded in 1846) and a grant of £490 was obtained from the £20,000 set aside for school building by the government. The Free School was demolished and a new school built on the site 'in the stile of one of the wings of Cobham Hall' at the suggestion of the Earl of Darnley. The architect was William Tierney Clark. The school provided for both boys and girls like the National School. The Free School had been for boys only.

St Thomas's Almshouses, *c.* 1880. The weatherboard almshouses were demolished and replaced by these buildings in about 1838. They are in similar style to the King Street Schools and may be by W. Tierney Clark, although there is a drawing in the Colyer Fergusson Album in the Kent Archaeological Library at Maidstone for Gravesend almshouses by Herbert Austen with them grouped around a courtyard. This version was never built.

*Left:* King Street frontage of the almshouses, with Glover & Homewoode sale bills and the cab rank in front, 1898. The original almshouses in Wrotham Road (now being rebuilt) were built with the proceeds of sale.

*Below:* King Street, *c.* 1902–3. On the left is Bryant & Rackstraws, drapers, next to them Caddel's printers and booksellers, founded in 1811, and beyond them Jacksons, cash drapers. The latter shops were both later absorbed by Bryant & Rackstraws. This site is now Woolworths. Next to King Street Schools are Tulks outfitters, later Dunn & Co., and the 'new' King's Head of 1895 (A.C. Smith, architect, W.M. Archer, builder). The electric tramway opened on 2 August 1902 and the cars originally had oil headlamps, the clips for which can be seen in this view. A single overhead wire was used which caused trouble at loops and was soon replaced by two.

King Street, *c.* 1905. The London County Bank (now National Westminster) was built on part of the almshouses site in 1898. It was a pleasant building in the 'Arts and Crafts' Baroque style by Alfred Williams, in red brick with Ancaster stone dressings. In 1903 David Greigs, grocers, built next door in a similar style. This building is now part of the bank. The one-man demi-tram which operated on the Windmill Street branch to the Old Prince of Orange can be seen. The fare was ¹□₂*d.*

King Street, *c.* 1935. Barclays Bank (now Woolwich Building Society) and Williamson's Café (now Abbey National Building Society) replaced the King Street Schools, the site of which was sold in 1932 to provide funds towards building the new St George's Schools in Meadow Road, opened in February 1939. An island in the middle of the road has replaced the tramway but David Greigs are still next to the Westminster Bank.

A trip up Windmill Street to the Railway Fruit Stores on the corner of Railway Place, *c.* 1890. For many years from 1920 the proprieter was William Ramsey, whose brother was manager of Dicks, the boot and shoe shop in High Street.

Princess Beatrice arriving at the Central station in 1893 to open the new municipal Day School, later the County School.

Milton Hall Stores, *c.* 1890. At this time it was run by the well-known grocer and provision merchant, John Adlington Mason. The building had started life as Tulley's Bazaar in 1835. Holiday-makers were welcome and there was a band. Round the sides were illuminated views of Italy and Switzerland. Refreshments and souvenirs were for sale and concerts held in the evening. Later it was used as the Drill Hall for the local Artillery Volunteers with a small cannon outside. After its use as the stores it became Unwins off-licence and then a furniture store. It is now empty.

The west side of Windmill Street, *c.* 1905. The white painted stucco building on the north corner of Sheppey Place on the left had a date shield on it with '1849'. This site is now car parks for the municipal offices.

A musical evening at the home of Mr and Mrs Lewis Gilbert, 120 Windmill Street, *c.* 1905 (photograph and information from the late Mr S. Garlick). From left to right: Mrs Lewis Gilbert, a French Huguenot (in the original photograph her husband was standing behind her); Alexander Henderson, uncle of Mr Garlick; Mrs Fidge from 118 Windmill Street (standing); Mr Bailey; Mr Blandford (?); Ernest Gilbert, with violin; Edith Fidge, Mrs Fidge's daughter, who became an opera singer and married an Italian Cadermontre (?); Charles Gilbert; Gertie Fidge, Charles' first wife, who died in childbirth; Doris Gilbert; her husband, Lewis Gilbert junior.

*Above:* The gates and railings of South House, Windmill Street, *c.* 1950. These came from the Town Pier (see p. 28) and have the borough arms on the left-hand gate support. Those at North House were similar. They were excluded from the wartime requisition of all gates and railings for iron but both have now been destroyed.

*Left:* Milton Congregational Church, Lacey Terrace (now Clarence Place), *c.* 1880 (Gravesend Library). It was erected in 1873 (architect, John Sulmar of London) and was intended to have a south-west tower. It was built as the result of a split in the Princess Street Chapel (see p. 43) congregation. It closed in 1955 and became a warehouse. In 1968 it became a Sikh Temple for the Indian community, who had previously used 55 Edwin Street. Lacey Terrace derived its name from Edward Lacey, a local builder and one-time mayor, who built a row of houses adjoining the church and lived at Baynard Castle, eventually going bankrupt.

The windmill on Windmill Hill, *c.* 1880. Then in use as a lookout for the local holiday-makers with a camera obscura on top, it was pulled down in 1894. The adjoining cottages and the Belle Vue Tavern burnt down on Mafeking night, 1900.

This is said to be one of the arches erected to welcome Princess Beatrice on her visit to the town in 1893 to open the Municipal Day School (Gravesend Library). I wonder if this is so as it seems to read 'A Hero's Welcome' and might relate to troops returning from the Boer War. The wall of Portland Villas can be seen on the left and in the extreme distance the gable end of the Old Prince of Orange is visible above the crown of the hill.

The architect's drawing for Portland Hall at the junction of Windmill Street and Leith Park Road. John Morris & Son of Poplar were the architects. It was started by Aspdin the Portland cement manufacturer in 1850 but work stopped in 1852 before the interior was finished. Efforts to sell by his creditors failed and finally the main portion was pulled down, leaving the rear wing which became a private dwelling house in about 1859, later known as West Hill House.

West Hill House just before it was demolished to make way for West Hill Place and a housing development, 1967. There are still some remains of the wall that Aspdin built round his estate, which extended from Portland Villas to Sandy Bank Road. (For Old Prince of Orange, Old Road, see p. 124).

This building on the west side of Stone Street was erected in 1800 as a hall for the Oddfellows Friendly Society. Later it became a Baptist Church before the Baptist congregation moved to Windmill Street in 1843. According to the *Gravesend Magazine* a total immersion font still existed in the building in 1911, long after it had become a builders' merchants. For many years, from 1912, the building was used by P.E. Liner & Co. and later, for a few years, by Olby. In 1867 it was a Primitive Methodist church until their move to the building in Darnley Street which still exists. Before 1912 it was used to show early films and had also been a hay and fodder merchants. It was demolished in about 1970 to make way for the Anglesea Centre.

This yard on the west side of Stone Street was originally the Borough Mews from which Clark's horse bus ran to Meopham in the 1890s. It belonged to J.C. Aylen, who was a well-known cyclist and member of the North Kent Cycle Club. Later it was J. Barty's Central Garage and, after housing a billiard saloon, it became part of P.E. Lines & Co. and Olby. The site is now part of the Anglesea Centre.

Alfred Joseph Clark's horse bus at Meopham, *c.* 1905. It left Meopham Green on Monday, Wednesday and Friday at 9.30 a.m. for the Borough Mews, returning at 1.30 p.m. Passengers could do their shopping and have their goods sent to the bus by 1.30. On Saturday there was an extra trip that left Meopham at 6.30 p.m., returning at 9.30 p.m. On Tuesday and Thursday there was a bus at 9.15 a.m. from Meopham via Sole Street and Cobham which returned from Gravesend at 2 p.m. The fare from Meopham or Sole Street to Gravesend was 8*d*, and to Cobham 6*d*. This bus later became a coffee stall in a field opposite the Tollgate and was destroyed by a bomb in the Second World War.

St Luke's Church, Wrotham Road, *c.* 1900 (Gravesend Library). Built as a Mission church to St James in 1890 (architect, Bassett-Smith), it survived for worship until about 1939, after which it was used as a church hall. It was demolished in about 1960 and the site is now a welfare clinic.

Entrance to Woodlands Park, *c.* 1938. In 1884 George Wood, the East Street brewer, built a new house which he called Woodlands, now the hotel. After his death, the council bought the land adjoining, known as Wood's Meadow, previously called Wellington's Orchard and Gravesend Orchard. They laid this out as a park with tennis courts and a bowling green. The gates were erected as a memorial to George V and opened with a golden key by Mayor Henry Alfred Hodge on 12 May 1937. The architect was the late Maurice Fuller, then assistant borough engineer, and the builder was the late William Hopkins.

Opening of Huggins Bungalows, 29 April 1922 (*Kent Messenger*). Generally known as Tipperary Cottages, they were built as almshouses for wounded soldiers of the First World War. The money was raised by Mrs Huggins, whose husband Alderman H. Huggins was Mayor 1914–16, with a series of Tipperary fairs. The site was given by Sir Thomas Colyer-Ferguson of Womball Hall and Ightham Mote as a memorial to his son Lt T.R. Colyer-Ferguson (inset), Gravesend's first VC, who was killed at the battle of Loos on 31 July 1917. In the centre is the Mayor, Alderman W.E. Thomas, and to his left Alderman Huggins, with top hat. To his right is probably H.H. Brown, town clerk, in bowler hat, and the Mace Bearer standing. Lord Desborough opened the bungalows. Is he the figure in the bowler hat to the Mayor's right? Sir Thomas and Lady Colyer-Ferguson appear to be the couple to the right. According to the *DNB*, Lord Desborough (formerly William Henry Glenfell) was 'Athlete Sportsman and public servant'. He was, at the time, War Minister and had lost two sons in the 1914–18 war.

*Left:* High Street, *c.* 1903. The upper end of High Street was half the width of the present carriageway, which was only widened when Bryant & Rackstraws drapers on the right was pulled down to make way for the present Woolworths in 1957. On the left is the New Prince of Orange (Burtons since 1928), built in 1805 after the Carpenter's Arms had been pulled down for the New Road in 1801. Before that there was a continuous row of buildings from the west side of High Street to the west side of Windmill Street (then known as Upper High Street). King Street at that time curved into High Street.

*Below:* A two-horse tram picking up passengers in New Road at the top of High Street. The horse tramway opened in 1883, originally with five small one-horse single-deck cars, but these were replaced by four double-deck two-horse cars in 1898, of which this is one. Note the adverts for Barkways, the Northfleet brewery, Rosherville Gardens and John Rose the tailors in High Street.

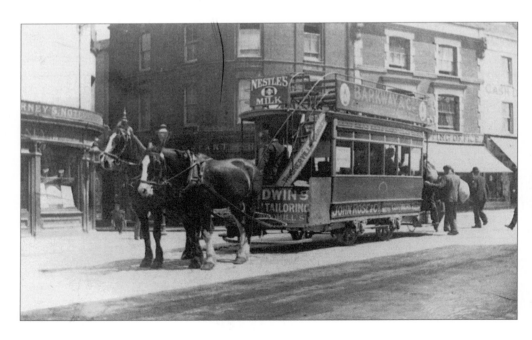

The Nelson Tap corner of Stone Street and New Road, with the Nelson Inn and first floor gallery and the stables in between, 1875. To the left can be seen Caddells Jacksons and King Street Schools. A borough policeman stands on the left at the entrance to Princes Street. The road was widened in 1876 when the new Nelson was opened in 1878 (closed 1983 and now McDonalds). The Nelson was formerly the Flower de Luce, 1528–1775, then the Marquis of Granby, 1775–1806.

Gravesend, 1817 (from a watercolour in the Gravesend Library). This is a view from the then recently cut New Road across the fields, with St George's Church on the right and the barn this side of it. To the left of the church can be seen Church House and other buildings in Church Street. The farm land in the foreground was developed with Wakefield Street, Kemthorne Street and Moscow Road in the 1830s.

*Above:* The chemist's shop at the junction of Princes Street and New Road, *c.* 1890. At that time Sharmans, later Rossiters, Moores, and finally Bolts, the site was incorporated in the new Marks & Spencer.

*Left:* Bolts the chemist's shop, surrounded by Marks & Spencer, *c.* 1960.

The new Marks & Spencer building, *c.* 1960. The 1927 façade of Marks & Spencer is still *in situ* with the old British Home Stores (formerly Missings) next door.

New Road looking west, *c.* 1925. The gentleman with the top hat to the right is probably one of a small group of buskers who played at the top of Princes Street and then went round with a hat. Next to Moores the chemist were George Atkins a fruiterer (formerly Nelson's the butchers) and Alfred Bond oil and colour-man. The large building next door, Missings drapers and toy store, later became the British Home Stores, which has now been completely rebuilt.

New Road looking east, *c.* 1893. Next to Bonds, George Missing had a tobacconist and his wife a fancy repository and registry office for servants. Next to this was George Saunders, a boot manufacturer, 'Our Boot Stores' then Coombes, seedsman and florist, and at Nos 10 and 11 the Misses H. Missing ran a confectionery store and bazaar. All these provided the site for Missings drapers, whose new shop opened in about 1905.

The offices of Messrs Tolhurst Lovell & Church, solicitors, No. 77 New Road, *c.* 1904. Known as the 'flat iron' because of its triangular shape, it was only wide enough for a WC at the east end adjoining Garden Row.

The new offices of the then Messrs Tolhurst Son & Church (77 New Road) were built in 1906 by Alfred Tolhurst, who also built the bank for Capital and Counties (architect, George Clay senior). The old offices had stood in the front garden and were only demolished when the firm moved into the new ones. The bank in due course became Lloyds, and the whole building was demolished in 1973 to make way for the Anglesea Centre and a new Lloyds Bank building.

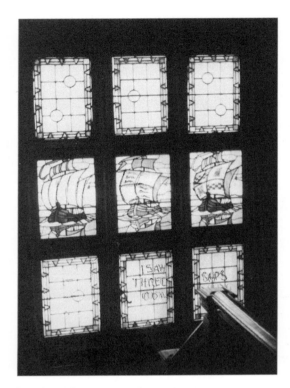

*Left:* The stained glass window on the stairs of the offices came from the old East India Company's office. It was destroyed when the premises were demolished in 1973.

*Below:* Garden Row, west side, *c.* 1930 (Llyd Roberts watercolour, Gravesend Library). Most of the row was demolished in about 1932, but the two brick cottages on the left remained until the area was cleared for the Anglesea Centre in 1973. Garden Row ran at right angles to New Road and then made a sharp turn to come out in Stone Street.

The weatherboard house at the rear of 77 New Road and the bank. Before the car park was laid out there had been a paved way from New Road to this house, which was occupied by the market gardener who cultivated the area before the construction of the railway. There was formerly a second row of cottages behind Garden Row and it was the entrance to this which caused the peculiar shape of the old office.

The front or south side of the same building. This was when it was used as offices by Hopkins the builders. It was at one time used as the stationmaster's house after the railway was built.

The offices of Messrs Rayner & Bridgeland, architects and surveyors, at 16 New Road, *c.* 1890. They later became the offices of H. Austen Clark & Son, chartered accountants, with a dry-cleaners underneath.

*Below:* E.C. Paine, grocer and provision merchant, 22–3 New Road, and G.C. King, draper, at 24–5 New Road, *c.* 1892. The drapers had previously been E.C. Paine but was probably disposed of after the death of his first wife. The whole block had been erected by Paine in the 'Queen Anne Revival' style and was the first such premises in Gravesend, the builder being W.H. Archer.

*Right:* E.C. Paine was an alderman of the Gravesend Council and was Mayor in 1893 and 1894. He was involved in a number of local companies, such as the Public Halls, of which he was chairman, and the Kent and Essex Land House and General Investment Company. He was also active in the public library, the hospital, Ragged School and North Kent Building Society.

*Below:* New Road, looking east, *c.* 1893. At the left-hand side was H. Moore, the boot and shoe manufacturer, who also had premises in the High Street. The fishmonger at No. 41 was William Dinmore and next to this the higher-built brick block was Mrs Bates at Nos 39–40, who had a toy warehouse and fancy repository. In about 1909 No. 39 became the London 'Penny Bazaar', which was the original name of Marks & Spencer. It continued here until the premises at 3–4 New Road were opened in 1927.

New Road, looking east from the Sun, with one of the arches put up to welcome Princess Beatrice when she opened the Municipal Day School in 1893. These arches were decorated with General Gordon's Chinese flags which he had given to the Ragged School. The Sun is on the left with Moores, the boot and shoe shop, next door. From the 1920s for many years Jack Stores greengrocers and confectionery was found here. On the right is the old Wheatsheaf on the corner of Darnley Road.

The New Road, looking west, c. 1960. To the left is the Salvation Army's citadel, which was built in 1807 as the Theatre Royal by a Mr J. Trotter. It was given to the Salvation Army in 1883 by the then owner Mrs Ruddell. All this area was demolished in 1969 when Tesco was built on the site and the Salvation Army moved to The Grove. Beyond can be seen Simes, the seed merchants and garden centre. In the early nineteenth century it is said to have been a stables and coach house. It is now a taxi park.

The Sun at the corner of Bath Street and New Road just before it was demolished to make way for road widening and the Trustee Savings Bank, *c.* 1970. Built in 1811 when Thomas Bowles, who had had the Sun at what is now Echo Square, moved here, for over a hundred years it was held by members of the Upton family.

St James' Church, *c.* 1905. The dog cart in the centre is said to be Dr Pinching's, the top-hatted driver being his coachman and later chauffeur, Mr Mungeam. On the left is the Pelham Road tram which worked a shuttle service between St James' Church and the Pelham Arms. It is one of the large eight-wheel cars which were found to be too big and had all been sold by 1906. Note the two men chatting in the middle of the crossroads, undisturbed by traffic.

*Left:* St James' Church, *c.* 1890. Built in 1852 (architect, S.W. Dawkes), it was the parish church of Gravesend from 1952 (when St George's was closed) until 1968 when St George's was once more constituted the parish church. St James', where the inferior Victorian ragstone had begun to deteriorate, was then demolished. Joynes House (formerly Blue Circle House) now stands on the site of the church and that of the vicarage (which was to the west on Overcliffe) and adjoining houses.

*Below:* Junction of New Road and Bath Street, looking towards Overcliffe, Northfleet, *c.* 1903. The large building on the right is the Public Halls, built in 1880 as the Borough of Gravesend British Worksman's Halls. It was then taken over by a limited company (now in process of being wound up) as a hall for entertainment of various kinds. Winston Churchill spoke here on his Boer War experiences. It later showed films and became a cinema, in succession the London, Regent, Rivoli and finally the 954-seat Super with a five-unit organ with cascade-illuminated console Compton. It was opened by Anna Neagle on 16 September 1933 and became part of the ABC, closing on 23 November 1958. The horse charabanc is probably one of Lewis Solomon's from the Royal Mews in the New Road, possibly on an excursion to Cobham.

*Right:* The spire of St Mark's Church, Rosherville, *c.* 1890. The church was built by members of the Rosher family in 1855 (architects, H. and E. Rose). There was constant trouble with the ragstone and extensive repairs were carried out in 1896 by W. and C.A. Bassett-Smith, at which time the angels round the spire were removed. It was finally demolished in 1976 and a new church built on the same site by the Gravesend architects, George Clay Partnership, opened in 1977.

*Below:* The tower at the London Road entrance to Rosherville Gardens, *c.* 1925. Built in 1864, it originally had a chiming clock which had a carillon of nineteen bells by Gillett & Brand of Croydon. According to a guidebook of 1888, this carillon was 'unsurpassed in England'! The tower was sold when the gardens closed in 1899. When they reopened for a few years in 1903 the spaces where the clock faces had been were filled with glass. The tower survived until 1938 when Henleys acquired what was left of the gardens and demolished it. The clock was sold when the gardens were closed in the late nineteenth century.

Bootmans Mill on top of the cliffs at the end of Rural Vale, c. 1900, from a watercolour by the late Stuart Kean (now in my possession). The Red Lion works quarry with a horse pulling chalk trucks can be seen on the right. The mill was built in 1840 and, after being derelict for some years, was pulled down in 1916. Milling was carried on for some years before this by an auxiliary steam engine.

The Leather Bottle, Northfleet, c. 1802. This view is taken from a painting by Edward Best, who was the parish clerk. It had been in existence since 1710. Note the saw pit in the triangle of land between Dover Road and New Road (opened in 1801 and providing a direct road to Gravesend). The 'underdog' can be seen in the pit with the 'top dog' above. The 'underdog' was a dusty, thirsty job as a result of the sawdust. No doubt the Leather Bottle provided plenty of the very necessary liquid refreshment for this job!

The Leather Bottle from the north-west, *c.* 1905. Springhead Road is to the right and the small building on the left of the road, at the rear of the Leather Bottle, was the old Northfleet lockup. In spite of its small size, it had a classical triangular pediment. When I lived opposite at 2 Springhead Road, as a small boy in the 1920s, it was occupied by a widow named Mrs Lubka, whose son Tommy had a glass eye. The gabled building and gates on the right were for J.B. Lingham's builders yard. He lived in the adjoining house, now part of the Granby Hotel.

London Road, looking east, *c.* 1905, showing one of the small three-window direct-stair trams, which replaced the large eight-wheel cars in 1905–6, waiting on the loop. To the left, in the chalk pit, is the end of the row of houses in Portland Road with the chimneys of the Imperial and Red Lion cement works. To the right is the projecting sign of the Leather Bottle and the long arm of the small single-deck demi-tram which worked the service between the Leather Bottle and the Pelham Arms. This photograph was probably taken from an upstairs window of 1 or 2 The Hill.

Northfleet church and Church Walk, again probably taken from a rear window of 1 or 2 The Hill, *c.* 1905. The photographer is looking across the corner of London Portland quarry. The tunnel leading to the works was below the buttresses and revetment, later replaced by a much larger tunnel for coal trains for the New Northfleet cement works (tunnel now disused). Church Path Cottages to the right were built in the early 1900s by Alfred Tolhurst. Next is St Botolph's School, the first part of which was built in 1838. In 1869 the infant school, to the left, was added. These schools were demolished when the new ones were opened in Dover Road in 1977 and the new vicarage now occupies the site of the old schools.

Northfleet Hill, looking west, *c.* 1895. On the left is P.G. Jennings (later F.J. Jones), the butcher's shop. The Queen's Head sign and Hill post office are opposite. The Coach and Horses and cottages adjoining can be seen in the centre. The large early eighteenth-century building on the left comprised Frederick Hancock, hairdresser, Frederick West, newsagent, and James Brown, the boot shop, and between them and the Coach and Horses was Alfred Terry, saddler, who also had premises in Gravesend. At the extreme left of this row can be seen George Mitchell, tailor.

*Above:* The Hill, *c.* 1905. The large building, the roof of which can be seen on the left, was the purpose-built offices of the Northfleet UDC, later a Co-op stores when the council took over Northfleet House in 1920. To the right, with the long sun blind, is Northfleet Hill post office and other small shops. Russells, Gravesend brewery, always had one tram car advertising their wares, 'Shrimp Band Beers', with large shrimps painted on it as seen here. Pictures of their public houses where this beverage could be obtained appeared in the fan lights on the lower deck.

*Right:* An end view of the Dove beside the lych-gate to Northfleet church. Built in about 1766, it burnt down in 1906 and was demolished the following year.

*Above:* Northfleet church (St Botolph's), *c.* 1890. It is seen from what was the Northfleet football ground before the chalk was quarried by London Portland cement works. At this time the building was covered with ivy. The Norman tower fell in 1628 and the present one was built in 1717 inside the ruins of the old one, part of the old wall being used to make steps up to the new tower entrance. The rebuilding was a curious mixture of brick and the old rubble. The little cottage to the left is said to have been moved here from the dockyard and was at one time occupied by the beadle. When Northfleet FC were playing at home they used to change in a shed behind the Leather Bottle and run along Church Path up to the pitch.

*Left:* The brass of Peter de Lacey in Northfleet church, *c.* 1805. This picture is probably from a drawing by Thomas Fisher of the Society of Antiquaries. He was rector (*sic*) of Northfleet 1356–75 and was secretary and receiver to Edward the Black Prince and clerk to the Keeper of the Privy Seal as well as holding other important offices. His brass was ripped off its original slab of blue marble at the 'restoration', turned round and placed on a new yellow stone with a new inscription and the canopy discarded. For a further description of this and the many 'lost' brasses of Northfleet, see *Archaeologia Cantiana,* vol. XXXII (1917, p. 38).

The vicarage, Northfleet, *c*. 1960. This picture was taken shortly before it was demolished and Vicarage Close was built on the site in 1961–2. It had been built in 1834 when Richard Keats was appointed vicar. His predecessors had been absentees and the previous vicarage on this site had been empty since 1764 except for brief periods. The so called 'Rectory House' at Snaggs Bottom was never the incumbent's residence but that of the farmer of the Rectorial Titles, in lay hands since the Reformation.

Infants from Lawn Road School processing along the High Street for Edward VII's Memorial Services at the Northfleet Recreation Ground, May 1910. I think this may be St. Botolph's Infant School as the figure appears to be S. Tiley, the headmaster of this school!

*Left:* Northfleet High Street Board Schools, *c.* 1925. They were built in 1886, the first Board Schools in Northfleet, and were expanded in 1891 to accommodate a further 500 pupils. The clock tower was built in 1887 as a memorial to Queen Victoria's Golden Jubilee (like the Gravesend clock tower). The school closed in 1986, and the upper part of the tower and clock were blown down in the hurricane of 15–16 October 1987 and the site was cleared.

*Below:* The Factory Club, Northfleet High Street, *c.* 1905. Built by Mr Bevan the cement manufacturer in 1878 for his cement workers (architects, Parr & Strong), it had a fine organ and hall in which concerts and other functions were held and was, for many years, a club. Now closed, the premises are believed to be on the market.

Northfleet High Street, looking west from the corner of Factory Road, *c.* 1925. Before 1869 it was known as Bow Street after a large house built by Major Wadham. When no tenant could be found it was let out in tenements and known as 'Paddy Wadham's Folly'. The shop just beyond the Factory Club was occupied by E. Rayner, oil, ironmongery and hardware. The business was later carried on by his three sons, Arnold, Eric and Ken Rayner, until the premises were taken over for redevelopment by the Northfleet UDC, which built Rayners Court. The last of the three, Arnold, died in 1997.

Northfleet High Street, looking east from College Road, 1895. The lines of the final horse tram terminus can be seen in the foreground. Messrs Church & Clinch, drapers, are on the left, with Northfleet post office a little further up just beyond the row of houses. Opposite was the Coopers Arms.

Plough Pond, *c.* 1905. As the pond is empty the sluice-gates on the left are no doubt open. It was fed by the Ebbsfleet and emptied into the Creek. The figure on the left is said to be S. Honeycombe, the Northfleet UDC surveyor, apparently inspecting the pond. At the rear is the Plough public house with the spire of Huggens College on the hill. Stonebridge Hill is to the right.

A view from Plough Marsh, showing Huggens College Almshouses on the skyline with the Plough below and the road ascending Stonebridge Hill before any of the houses were built, *c.* 1890. What appears to be the Ebbsfleet, or perhaps flooding, crosses the middle distance.

A view from an aeroplane, looking across the New Northfleet Paper Mills, formerly the Ekman Pulp and Paper Co., *c.* 1930. Most of the works were in fact in Swanscombe parish and All Saints' Church can be seen in the right-hand corner. Karl Ekman, a Swede, invented the sulphite process of making paper from wood pulp. There is a memorial to him in Northfleet churchyard. To the left, on the waterside, can be seen Britannia Metals and to the right the deep-water wharf used by the paperworks but formerly Kirby's chalk and lime. It was used by various small cement works, including the Britannia, the chimneys of which can be seen in the middle distance. All the small works in this area had long since closed.

Hall Road near the present Hall Road Schools, *c.* 1910.

*Above:* A North Kent omnibus, *c.* 1915. In 1913 the tramway company built a bus depot adjoining their tram sheds and offices in Fiveash Road and started to operate services between Gravesend and Dartford and Chatham. This is a First World War picture with a lady conductor. I remember these Daimlers in the 1920s, then operated by Maidstone & District (when the modern buses with pneumatic tyres were Tilling-Stevens Electro petrol with solid tyres). One could sit on the bench seat beside the driver (if my mother was in a good mood and she usually was), the fares being collected through a small window. My memory of the General Strike, aged five, is of not being allowed to sit beside the drivers, who were then volunteers with a special constable sitting at the other end of the seat!

*Left:* A Leyland low roof Titan bus, 1929. Sixteen of these replaced the trams on 1 March 1929. At first in red with the BET wheel and magnet symbol on the sides, they were operated by Maidstone & District who soon repainted them green with the M & D logo until taken over by London Transport in 1933.

# CHAPTER THREE

# THE OLD ROAD

*Between the Lion Garage, Chalk and the Leather Bottle, Northfleet, there was formerly a main road, now the B261, which appears on Symonson's map of 1596 and is thought to be earlier than the A226 which ran to the waterside for the Long Ferry to London and then, before the building of the New Road in 1801, by various routes across the Chalk Cliff to Northfleet. The course of the B261 may have been dictated before the sea wall was built, when the river at high tide may have flowed up the now dry valley by Milton church and prevented a route nearer the river. Known as the Old Dover Road and in some documents as the 'London to Paris Road' it is now Old Road, East and West in what was Gravesend and Dover Road East and Dover Road in Northfleet. A number of pictures I had hoped to use here have not proved suitable for reproduction but I have included some of Singlewell Road and of the area now covered by the Girls' Grammar School. The Leather Bottle is dealt with on pp. 111–12, under the Main Road.*

The Lion Garage, *c.* 1924 (Gravesend Library). The Lion Garage and Arnold Transport were begun by Francis ('Fingey') Arnold, son of Bernard Arnold, who owned Milton Hall after his father's death in 1909 until his own in 1925. Two of the Arnold Lions can be seen in front of the garage and still remain in the forecourt of the present garage. The land was formerly the most easterly point of the Milton Hall Estate Meadow. (For a brief history of the Arnold family see my article in the *Gravesend Historical Society's Transactions* No. 35, 1989.) Francis Arnold lived at Hartley.

Christ Church, Old Road East, 1938. Christ Church was moved to this site in 1934, the building on its former site in Parrock Road, surrounded by Christ Church Crescent, having become unsafe and the town having spread to the south. It was consecrated by the Rt Revd Martin Lynton Smith, Lord Bishop of Rochester, on 14 September 1935, Holy Cross Day. He was probably the last of the 'aristocratic' Bishops of Rochester who always wore a shovel hat and gaiters and had an open Rolls-Royce; he usually sat in the front beside the chauffeur. He was an affable old boy whom I remember well from when I was a small boy at school at Rochester. The architect was George Clay and he added a clerestory to the nave and battlements to the tower.

The late Georgian coat of arms of *c*. 1802 was in the basement of 10 Old Road East in about 1925 when this room was Charles Gilbert's museum in the house he had built. It still remains, apparently gesso work, and was probably a 'George' from a public house. The Old Prince of Orange was the George in 1633 according to Mr Green but the dates do not agree, although I was told it came from the Old Prince when it was demolished in 1932 (by an unreliable witness who had no personal knowledge).

The Windmill Street tram at the Old Prince of Orange, *c.* 1925. The conductor is said to be Mr W. Tate. Note the car at the left which had probably been buying petrol at the side door of the Prince where there was a hand-cranked pump and a large old wooden shed with oil and spare parts. A sign 'Petrol' informed motorists using the Old Road as a bypass for the town centre that supplies were available. This is one of the small open-top trams had replaced the one-man demi-car for this service from about 1915 and the fare was 1*d* single and 1¹⍰₂*d* return.

Old Prince of Orange from Old Road West, *c.* 1845. At this time donkeys were the favourite means of transport up Windmill Street. They could be hired from stables near the present railway bridge for 6*d* return and it is recorded that they would not proceed beyond the Prince under any circumstances or inducements. At a later stage the Prince was the end of the 1*s* fare for local cabs; anywhere beyond cost 1*s* 6*d*.

Singlewell Road looking south, c. 1900. This corner was always known as 'Hammond's Corner' after the bakery and shop on the right which were founded by Mr Humphrey Hammond in 1884, when the shop and row of cottages were built by Alfred Tolhurst on his Littlemead Estate. He had previously managed the shop later occupied by Mr Frank Smith in Milton Road. After his death it was carried on by his son Herbert Charles Hammond and two daughters Annie and Daisy who looked after the shop, which sold sugar sticks and a little confectionery as well as bread, the loaves being sometimes specially baked to suit the customer's tastes. Herbert Charles, always known as 'Bertie', who delivered bread from a three-wheeled tricycle, died in 1967, aged eighty-five. His sister Daisy predeceased him in her eighties, but Annie continued to live on the premises until her death in 1975, aged ninety-nine. The row of houses opposite is Warwick Terrace, built in 1898 on part of the playing field of Clarence House (at one time Gutteridge's) School, which had a small pavilion here. Note the horse-drawn pantechnicon, probably Coopers, unloading furniture. As late as 1926 my parents had one of these to move from Northfleet to Upper Singlewell Road.

A view from the back window of one of the houses in Cross Lane East before the Gravesend Land Company laid out the eastern ends of Portland Avenue, Ferndale Road, Malvina Avenue, Smarts Road and Northridge Road, c. 1920. (Mrs Valerie Martin) The building on the left was Dalton's smallholding where he sold fruit and vegetables. The allotments are those laid out during the First World War when people were encouraged to grow their own vegetables. All this area was shortly to be laid out for housing and built on in the 1920s and 1930s.

The Mid-Kent Golf Club, 1909. The land between Singlewell Road and Wrotham Road was laid out as an eighteen-hole course in 1908/9, largely due to the efforts of Mr C.E. Hatton the secretary, and was opened on 26 November 1909 by the Rt Hon. A.J. Belfour MP and the Hon. A. Lyttelton MP, who were partnered by James Braid and Harry Vardon, two famous ex-champions. The club house (shown here) was originally on the east side of the road, at the corner of what is now Ascot Road, and the course extended down Singlewell Road to the cottages, the first hole being in a northerly direction. This part of the course was used for allotments in the First World War and was thereafter developed for building when Dennis Road, The Fairway and Hillingdon Road were cut.

The Mayor, Councillor H.E. Davis JPCC, and Mayoress distributing Coronation medals to schoolchildren in 1911. This was once the playing field of the Gravesend Ormonde Football Club, which later amalgamated with the Gravesend Town Club to become Gravesend United. The Girls' County School (now the Grammar School) was erected on this site in 1926. The backs of the houses in Old Road West and on the corner of Pelham Road can be seen. The supports for the stand came from the long bar at Rosherville Gardens.

# Other titles published by The History Press

### Haunted Kent
JANET CAMERON

Including heart-stopping accounts of apparitions, manifestations and related supernatural phenomena, Haunted Kent contains new and well-known spooky stories from around the county.

£9.99   978 0 7524 3605 0

### Deal and District at War
DAVID COLLYER

Richly illustrated, *Deal and District at War* recounts many unique and controversial events which include: a German coastal raid in Sandwich Bay when at least 1 British soldier was snatched and the world-famous 'Lifeboat Doctor' James Hall. This book will evoke powerful memories for those whose families experienced the war and provide fascinating reading for anyone interested in the history of Deal and District.

£14.99   978 0 7524 4953 1

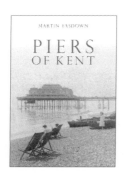

### Piers of Kent
MARTIN EASDOWN

Kent was once at the forefront of the British seaside resorts, and this book concentrates on the construction of piers along the coastline of Kent.

£12.99   978 0 7524 4220 4

Visit our website and discover thousands of other History Press books.
**www.thehistorypress.co.uk**